THE FRILLED SHARK

By Sara Green

BELLWETHER MEDIA · MINNEAPOLIS, MN

Jump into the cockpit and take flight with Pilot books. Your journey will take you on high-energy adventures as you learn about all that is wild, weird, fascinating, and fun!

This edition first published in 2013 by Bellwether Media, Inc.

No part of this publication may be reproduced in whole or in part without written permission of the publisher. For information regarding permission, write to Bellwether Media, Inc., Attention: Permissions Department, 5357 Penn Avenue South, Minneapolis, MN 55419.

Library of Congress Cataloging-in-Publication Data

Green, Sara, 1964-
The frilled shark / by Sara Green.
    pages cm. – (Pilot. Shark fact files)
Audience: 8-12.
Summary: "Engaging images accompany information about the frilled shark. The combination of high-interest subject matter and narrative text is intended for students in grades 3 through 7"– Provided by publisher.
Includes bibliographical references and index.
ISBN 978-1-60014-869-9 (hardcover : alk. paper)
1. Frilled shark–Juvenile literature. I. Title.
QL638.95.C4G74 2013
597.3'4–dc23
                        2012031235

Printed in the United States of America, North Mankato, MN.

TABLE OF CONTENTS

FRILLED SHARK
IDENTIFIED

   A large fishing boat cruises slowly off the coast of Japan. It sweeps a **trawl** along the bottom of the deep ocean. At the end of the day, fishers pull the heavy net into the boat. As they inspect the day's catch, they discover an odd-looking fish. At first they think they have caught an eel. Then they study the fish more carefully. It has a small **dorsal fin** and frilly **gill slits**. It is a frilled shark!

   The fishers are thrilled to see this uncommon fish up close. They quickly toss it back into the ocean, where it will swim back to deeper waters. Who knows if they will ever see a frilled shark again!

Frilled sharks inhabit the cool coastal waters of the Atlantic, Pacific, and Indian Oceans. They have even been found in the very cold waters off the northern coast of Norway. Frilled sharks usually swim near **continental shelves** at depths between 400 and 4,200 feet (120 and 1,280 meters).

UNEXPECTED CATCH

Japanese fishers brought up the first frilled shark from deep waters in the late 1800s. They called it a lizard shark at first because of its strange appearance.

☐ = frilled shark territory

N
W ✦ E
S

frilled shark

human

Frilled sharks are medium in size. The average male is between 3 and 4 feet (1 and 1.2 meters) long. Females are larger. Their average length is between 4 and 5 feet (1.2 and 1.5 meters). The largest frilled sharks can measure over 6 feet (1.8 meters) long.

The frilled shark is one of the oldest shark species alive today. It is considered a **living fossil**. This means it has many of the same physical characteristics as sharks that lived 200 million years ago. The frilled shark has a small dorsal fin and an **anal fin** set far back on its body. These fins help the shark stay balanced. Two short **pectoral fins** shaped like paddles allow the shark to steer. The frilled shark moves forward when it sways its long, wispy **caudal fin** from side to side.

dorsal fin

caudal fin

anal fin

The frilled shark has a slinky brown body, a rounded snout, and a large mouth. Most modern types of sharks have five pairs of gill slits. The frilled shark has six. The gills wrap around the shark's throat like a frilly collar. Unlike most modern sharks, the frilled shark's snout does not extend over its mouth. Instead, its mouth is located at the front of its head.

MONSTERS OF THE DEEP

Frilled shark sightings may have inspired people to believe in sea serpents.

pectoral fin

FRILLED SHARK
TRACKED

Frilled sharks are **ovoviviparous**. Babies develop in eggs inside the mother's body. As they grow, they receive food from a **yolk sac** attached to their bodies. The frilled shark may have a **gestation time** that lasts more than 3 years. This is one of the longest gestation times in the animal kingdom. Mothers then give birth to 2 to 12 pups. The average litter size is 6. At birth, each pup measures between 16 and 24 inches (40 and 60 centimeters).

Frilled sharks **mature** slowly. Most are fully grown before they can reproduce. Researchers suspect that mature frilled sharks seek mates year-round. However, they still do not know how long frilled sharks live.

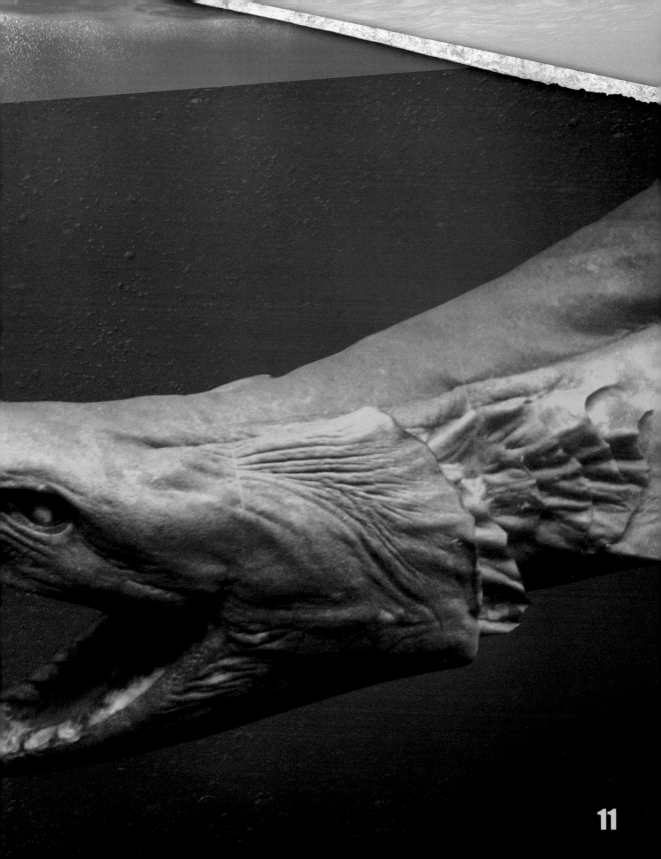

The frilled shark has a mouthful of small needle-sharp teeth arranged in rows. About 25 separate rows fill both the upper and lower jaws for a total of nearly 300 teeth. Each tooth has three sharp points that curve inward. The pointy teeth are like hooks that trap squids and octopuses, the frilled shark's favorite prey. A variety of fish, including other sharks, are also on the menu. The frilled shark opens its jaws wide to swallow prey larger than itself.

13

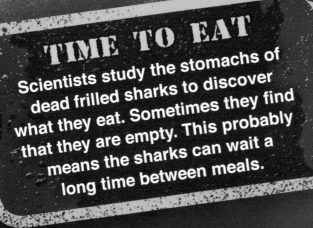

TIME TO EAT

Scientists study the stomachs of dead frilled sharks to discover what they eat. Sometimes they find that they are empty. This probably means the sharks can wait a long time between meals.

Because of its deep-sea habitat, little is known for sure about the frilled shark's eating habits. Scientists believe that it hunts for prey along continental shelves and in underwater caves. **Lateral lines** along the shark's body help it detect the movements of prey. A large oil-filled liver keeps the shark **buoyant** and allows it to float motionless.

When prey swims near, the frilled shark is thought to strike like a snake. Its gill slits may close to help the shark suck prey into its mouth. The shark then uses all of its teeth to grasp the slippery food. Instead of chewing its meal, the frilled shark likely swallows prey whole.

Frilled sharks are considered harmless to people. They swim in waters too deep for swimmers and divers. People rarely encounter them in their natural habitat. The only injuries caused by frilled sharks are accidental. A few scientists have cut their hands on the sharp teeth as they examined the sharks in research labs. Those who handle frilled sharks must be careful!

FRILLED SHARK
CURRENT STATUS

Nobody knows how many frilled sharks live in the ocean. No matter the number, most experts believe that deep-sea fishing could be a threat to this shark. Frilled sharks can end up as **bycatch** on lines and in trawls meant for other fish. They are either thrown back into the ocean or used for their meat.

Many scientists worry that this rare shark is especially at risk because it does not reproduce often. For this reason, the International Union for Conservation of Nature (IUCN) has given the frilled shark a **near threatened** rating.

SHARK BRIEF

Common Name: Frilled Shark

Also Known As: Frill Shark

Lizard Shark

Scaffold Shark

Claim to Fame: Frilly gill slits and
eel-like appearance

Hot Spots: Japan

Taiwan

Scotland

Norway

Life Span: Unknown

Current Status: Near Threatened (IUCN)

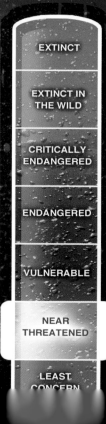

EXTINCT

EXTINCT IN
THE WILD

CRITICALLY
ENDANGERED

ENDANGERED

VULNERABLE

NEAR
THREATENED

LEAST
CONCERN

Researchers still have much to learn about the frilled shark's life in the deep ocean. Because frilled sharks cannot live long in **captivity**, researchers must study their behavior in the wild. Diving into the deep waters where frilled sharks live is not easy. Researchers must be trained to use special equipment. They must also be able to tolerate swimming in dark, cold waters. The efforts are worthwhile. The more knowledge researchers gain, the more they will be able to protect one of the strangest animals in the world.

GLOSSARY

anal fin—the fin close to the tail fin on the underside of a fish

buoyant—able to float

bycatch—animals that are accidentally caught with fishing nets or lines

captivity—any environment that does not allow an animal total freedom

caudal fin—the tail fin of a fish

continental shelves—flat underwater extensions of continents that drop to the ocean floor

dorsal fin—the fin on the back of a fish

gestation time—the time it takes young to develop inside the mother

gill slits—the openings on the sides of a fish's head through which water passes

lateral lines—a system of tubes beneath a shark's skin that helps it detect changes in water pressure

living fossil—a species that has changed little since prehistoric times

mature—to become old enough to reproduce

near threatened—could soon be at risk of becoming endangered

ovoviviparous—producing young that develop in eggs inside the mother's body; ovoviviparous animals give birth to live young.

pectoral fins—a pair of fins that extend from each side of a fish's body

trawl—a strong net that is dragged along the ocean floor

yolk sac—a sac of nutrients that feeds some animals as they develop inside their mothers

TO LEARN MORE

At the Library
Lynette, Rachel. *Bluntnose Sixgill Sharks and Other Strange Sharks*. Chicago, Ill.: Raintree, 2012.

Norwich, Grace. *Shark-a-Phobia*. New York, N.Y.: Scholastic Inc., 2011.

Wilsdon, Christina. *Sharks*. Pleasantville, N.Y.: Gareth Stevens Publishing, 2009.

On the Web
Learning more about frilled sharks is as easy as 1, 2, 3.

1. Go to www.factsurfer.com.

2. Enter "frilled sharks" into the search box.

3. Click the "Surf" button and you will see a list of related Web sites.

With factsurfer.com, finding more information is just a click away.

INDEX